*BEYOND
MY SKIN*

BEYOND MY SKIN

POETRY BY GRACE KARAM

PALMETTO
P U B L I S H I N G
Charleston, SC
www.PalmettoPublishing.com

Copyright © 2024 by Grace Karam

All rights reserved
No portion of this book may be reproduced, stored in a retrieval system, or transmitted in any form by any means–electronic, mechanical, photocopy, recording, or other–except for brief quotations in printed reviews, without prior permission of the author.

Paperback ISBN: 979-8-8229-2126-9

*Dedicated to my favorite reader, Cierra.
I hope you are in a cafe in Scotland reading these.
I love you.*

Table of Contents

That Intimate Light 1

THE SUN

A Stranger Lust 5
Girl Is Made of Fire 6
Daddy. 8
If I Could Stay Like This 10
Just Sit 11
Quieter 12
Pink Cyclops 13

THE MOON

Backyard Galaxy. 17
Phantom Queen. 18
Everywhere 19
I Am the Moon. 20
I Fell in Love 21
My Monster 22
Not Yet 24
Praying to the Moon 25
Wholly 26
Desert. 28

THE EARTH

As I Fell Asleep in Belfast. 31
A Time Gone 32
Coffee and Paper 33

Cold	34
Here	35
Lady New York	36
Morning and Night	37
Pink Suds	38
Sublime	40
Red Puff	42

BODY

Angry Woman	45
Body Spring	48
Losing My Strength Again	49
Oil Paint	50
She	51
Soft	52
Today	54
Tower	55
Trash Can	56
Womb	57

MIND

Insomnia	61
Invader	62
Passion	63
Psychological Flexibility	64
Self-Pity	65
Sad	66
Sticky	68
Therapy	69

Thinking	70
Unfocused	74
What Is Real?	75
Why Are You Here?	76

That Intimate Light

There are days when I wake up early, before life starts.
When my eyes are closed, the world is gone.
For all I know, it completely disappears, and I am floating in time and space.
And I'm alone.
But it is those moments of loneliness—
The time in the morning when it is neither night nor day, and the air is still—
When I am free to take up the space beyond my skin.
Gentle, young light shines through window glass,
Illuminating the tulle skirts of my princess dreams.
Life doesn't exist here like it does in the afternoon.
I get to dance with shadow friends, bent limbs
Entangled and pushed together.
I love that;
That mess of things that a tired brain cannot piece together.
Peace alone.

THE SUN

A Stranger Lust

She stands around the back
Searching faces and places and somewhere to exist fully
She is here and unaware of my dreaming eyes
A stitch within a larger frame but I see only her
I see the privilege of the sun
It cloaks her in gold and warms her skin
I grow jealous of the light and shadow
Weaving so intimately around her body
A dance I will not have
A touch I will not feel
And still a picture laid clear in my mind
A girl who I might kiss so tenderly upon her lips
Both pink and sweet
I cannot miss one second of her
I'd count minute after minute that I'd get
To spend with her hands interlaced with my own
And I fear the time my vision will end
And the realities of our separate worlds
Will take us away from each other
We are destined to blend away
Never meeting but always wondering
Did she see me too

Girl Is Made of Fire

The Sun is a god and my dad is the Sun.
He is a gaseous being, boiling and bursting with gaslights.
He created me from his fire and named me "Girl."
"Girl" was not supposed to have opinions.
"Girl" was not supposed to ask questions.
"Girl" was not supposed to fight back.
Because "Girl" was made to listen instead of speak.
Created to fill a void without plans of filling mine.
"Girl" lost her innocence.
"Girl" didn't listen.
"Girl" likes girls.

My dad is a god.
He likes to rule over me so I don't get hurt.
He tells me I have to be careful,
    So careful that I shouldn't do anything on my own.
My dad locked me in the bathroom with his words.
"Girl" cries and screams, and the Sun never hears it.
"Girl" is good at hiding herself.

How dare you!
How dare you tell me I'm wrong!
I'm a liar because I couldn't have made it here without your help?
That's what you said when you yelled at me for being more "Girl"
    than you wanted.
I guess even gods can't create perfection.
But you thought you could.

Is that why you lied to me?
You grand star that shines light on all my mistakes;
Is "Girl" not what you expected?
Because "Woman" is what you get now.
And "Woman" is ready to show herself.
"Woman" will not apologize.
"Woman" is made of fire.
"Woman" is a goddess after all.

Daddy

Dressed in red silk and velvet,
Tiny roses along my collar,
Sparkling water and a bouquet.
Princess who dreams up a hero,
A hero who knows how to fight,
A hero that must be protected
Because to see the hero hurting
Is like watching the sun darken.

Daddy slew monsters for me.
When I grew out of my princess clothes,
He told me sparkles and flowers were still important;
I was still important even though I changed.
It made him cry when the dress wouldn't fit.
So I mourned the love my hero once gave me
And welcomed the new.

When I changed, he changed.
He taught me the enemy's way.
He wanted me to stay in his kingdom,
Hidden and safe and seemingly happy.
Yet I longed for adventure.
I longed for trouble and regret,
And he told me he understood;
That he once longed for the same things.

Daddy saved me after I made my mistakes and never before.
He knew I had to hang on to my curiosity.
So he held my hand before I walked out the gate,
And made me promise to remember all he taught me.
He told me to hold my head up high.
Royalty doesn't slouch;
Royalty stays strong.
So that's what I'll be:
Royal and woman and hero.

If I Could Stay Like This

If I could stay like this:
In the dark with a pencil in hand and
A pink hue on the page from my dragon fruit candle,
I would most definitely drown in a romantic depression.
The kind of sadness that isn't yours, but you feel it anyway.
The way you empathize with a character in a book.
If being alone felt like this, I wouldn't cry anymore.
I would simply keep my eyes open in the flame
By my books and journals
And dread the morning that signals the continuing of time.
I'd love to be stuck in a scene and left to soak in all that it is.
When seconds pass by, I am the most lonely.
Without the sun telling time, I can be still
And pretend I don't have to move or perform to exist.
I simply sit and am.

Just Sit

Take my hand, quickly, we have to hurry!
Watch your step, these stairs are steep!
Inhale, almost there...
Exhale, one more step...

Finally!
Don't you see it?
Where the light shifts through the clouds?
It pushes past everything so it can shine on us.
Doesn't that make you feel warm?

Ignore the harsh winter breezes
Pulling at your hair and clothes.
It's not time to play.
Just sit and listen to the sun.
It's so beautiful above this dark place.

Quieter

I wonder if it's quieter up there.
I wonder if anyone's ever touched the clouds
And accidentally stolen some of the sunshine.

Maybe one day, that is where we will be.
It seems so much more peaceful than down here.
But what if we are upside down?

What if that peace is really below us,
And I can't see because of all the
Blood rushing to my head?

Pink Cyclops

Crinkle-cracked oats woke the wide-eyed dead
My bloodshot eyes scraped across each body
Made of silent vapor and time-worn rags
Each eyelid fluttering while I am still
Pitied creatures fail to see me real
Tangible, soft and breathing, sharp and warped inside,
They'd surely cloak me in green and soil
If only their ears buzzed when I called them
Outside the flying cage is a blinding heat
Isolated by the crowded seats
The light covers them in a blanket of roses and misses my skin
Pink—like the pink of my eyes, of tongues and sweet whispers,
Poisoned passion and toxic twilight trapped in flawed flesh
Escaped just over the violent horizon
While I still watch and still beg for someone to notice
I'm still lonely and still cold in all this sweat
Waiting to be colored like the sun
Like the moving lips of Them
And still the pink misses me
And still I am alone

THE MOON

Backyard Galaxy

She is made of the stars, and I am the moon
My dark home sparkles in her eyes
She is my twisted sister
My sister who knows my pain
And we hold hands as we bleed
So we know we aren't alone

I have a sister made of sunlight
She is bright and happy and cool
Intense and fiery, she is the golden child
Her bright light shows me who I am
We play to keep our smiles from dropping
And she tells me I'll be okay

He is made of soil and grass, the tide and the clouds
My brother comes from the earth
He is wise and complex
A collection of all of us
As I push him to take up space and show us who he is
He wonders about us each day

I am the moon
I cry with my siblings
And reflect light to their darkness
I pull and push until they feel loved
Together we twirl and morph
Dancing around each other for eternity

Phantom Queen

Black birds lined up on the wire of fate,
A funeral march of glittering wings,
A black parade to lead you to the gate.
The potential of their mystery sings.
They fly high, swirling like a backward clock.
Upon their dark feathers is an omen.
Carried like an infant, held by the flock,
A battle cry and something stolen.
A sign of war and blood, cold and heartless,
Success, mystery, and a sleeping death.
You drown in your own personal darkness
Like the suicide of Lady Macbeth.
Or the Morrigan's triple goddess glow
Swooping and shifting the lives of all men.
A warning sign of magic from below
To be delivered time and time again.
They hold messages tied to their black souls
Of lost lives, found trinkets, and silenced cries.
The ravens and crows and birds black as coal
Are the keepers of our fateful demise.
Grim reaper vultures carry your ghost
Cloaked in smoldering black mortality;
They hold secrets and never leave their post,
Wicked yet kind, they rule morality.
Your life laid out, an obsidian scene
Placing you at the feet of the Phantom Queen.

Everywhere

Anxiety lives in my chest.
It dwells in my stomach, making it quake.
It captures my hands so I am too weak to grab on to logic.
But depression?
Depression is everywhere.
It is my brain.
It is my mouth.
It makes up my skin and bones and blood.
All of me grows dreary.
Like the moon, I need someone to really see me.
To see how I'm drowning.
How I worry over everything and nothing all at once.
See me, and help me.
Because the water is starting to feel nice.

I Am the Moon

If I am the moon, then who are you?
A masculine brute like the sun?
A distant star, lonely among black nothingness?
Or are you down on earth, watching?
Waiting for my body to shift with the night?
Do you feel pulled to me?
Are you the grand tide that ties itself to me each day,
Tethered to me like a kite?
What would happen if you were to step outside,
Under my glowing figure,
And pray to be divine and cosmic?
If I could, I would grab you gently
And show you what it is to float and twirl
Around something as complex as humanity.
Would you dare to sit, cradled in my palm,
As I show you all this place has to offer?

I Fell in Love

I fell in love with a woman high above me
I do not deserve her time or her smile
But she gives it to me whenever I call
She is powerful and sublime
And she tells me she loves me by spelling it out in the night sky
She is luminous
She shines the light in my eyes
She makes up the wonder in my brain
And she never leaves me alone
I scream and cry and howl
So she knows I'm here for her too
I will always be here for her
And I will always love her
The way you're supposed to love something
As heavenly as the Moon

My Monster

I was born with a monster on my mouth, and she's never left my
 tongue.
I was born on a moonless night, and the first thing my mother did was
 weep at my hideous face,
Hidden by a purple-red tumor, taking space and attention from my
 labored breath.

There is a monster on my mouth, and surgery couldn't separate us.
Craving beauty, they cut and cut until my mouth was bare, and still my
 monster stayed.
Though they could not see her, she was just as loud and angry.

I have a monster on my mouth, and Mom and Dad don't like her.
They hated her for being me, so I smothered her with both of my
 hands in hopes that they'd shut up.
She cried when they sprinkled holy water on my head and when they
 said I was made to follow.
She held me when they made me cry and fought for me when they
 tore me down.
She took up space when they made me small and promised to love me
 when I couldn't.

She is the monster that lives on my mouth, invisible now but just as
 dark as that tumor.
When my body was no longer mine, she protected me from him.
She was screaming when he touched me and whispering when I
 couldn't be soft with myself.

She battled for me when they yelled threats from their cars and when
    they said it was my fault.
I think she is my strength.

The monster that lives on my mouth, the monster that I've become,
Has given me a voice that can say no.
A voice that can sing and cry and tell the truth
Even though all I've been taught is to stay silent.

Not Yet

Every night I lie awake and wait for Death to take me.
I never hear the buzzing flies
Or his carriage squeaking.
But I smell a stench,
Putrid and pungent,
Like garbage and decay.
He's close,
Watching over me,
Teasing me with eternal nothingness.
I wait by my window for
The ghost-white horses to strut from the darkness
And take me to my grave.
I tell myself I'm ready to go,
But as he makes me wait, I notice
Just how beautiful the moon is,
And I realize I will never see her again.
So I wait and wait with her, hoping I still have time
To soak in her feminine glow.
I can be nothing tomorrow.
Tonight I am simply a woman talking to the moon.

Praying to the Moon

I like to talk to the Moon.
I like to look up and breathe in
The air that shines with Her glow.
She is mysterious and kind,
And I tell Her my deepest secrets.
The ones that plague my brain.
I share dreams and nightmares
As She holds me in her feminine gaze.
I grow tired and peaceful.
Even in the darkness, I talk to Her
Because She is just as important when She hides.
But these days, when our sky seems Moonless,
She is there, wrapped in a deep black blanket.
I love Her the way you wish you loved your god.
I do not fear Her the way you fear your god.
I simply sit and stare and speak a language
Only She can understand.
So worship your god;
Stay devout to suffering.
I am simply resting my weary head
On the light the Moon reflects
As I pray to soak in all the cosmic femininity
She has to offer.

Wholly

I saw the Moon sleeping in the morning sky.
She snored so loudly I couldn't hear myself think.
So I whispered up a question, hoping she'd dream up an answer.
Her eyes fluttered at my voice:
"Is this who I'm meant to be?
Can I do this on my own?"

I saw the Moon resting in the morning sky,
And I told her I was doing fine.
That I was happy and fulfilled and free.
But she knows my mind too well.

I saw the Moon holding up the morning sky.
Her cracked silver hands pushing the clouds
And pulling the blue reflection of her oceans up like a blanket.
I told her how beautiful she was;
She told me she was a reflection of my spirit:
"You are meant for more than they say."

I saw the Moon, and I said hello and waited.
Her pearly figure stretched wide and white.
The crescent form morphed into a woman who looked like me.
Naked and sparkling, she floated down for a kiss.

"You are only a sliver of your full self."
I twirled around her fingers as her words sank in,
Tasted her pearl lips on mine,

And dreamed up a life of true freedom.
But the dream is only a dream,
And soon I will be in the same mundane life.

I saw the Moon dominate the morning sky.
I gripped the edges of the earth and jumped up to meet her gaze.
"Being alone doesn't mean you'll be lonely.
Being alone means being free to love yourself wholly."

Desert

The desert is a dreary place
Anger and heat shake hands
Dust and dirty water are our atmosphere
Waiting for rain to come but knowing
When it does it will be hot like everything else
Finally I feel a drop hit my shoulder
And another on my head,
Giving me a welcome chill
I am overjoyed at the weather
Until I see the red stains on my arms and legs
I wipe my face to see the truth
And I see blood pooled under my feet
Puddles of red collecting in the street
And our desert drowning in crimson tears
This is not coming from the clouds
A dark blood moon rises over my head
And swallows the pricking cacti
The tumbleweeds and lizards
Blow in the wake of each bloody breeze
And I am soaked in cosmic pain

THE EARTH

As I Fell Asleep in Belfast

As I fell asleep in Belfast, my consciousness lifted
As though I were a ghost,
Out of my body,
And traveled back to the ocean cliffs near the land of giants.
Along rope bridges and steep hills sprinkled with wildflowers,
I ventured aimlessly for the first time.
Finally, without a plan, I felt a sense of direction.
I wandered, floundered, tripped, and traveled along the spongy grass
And dared to dangle my tiny feet
Over the rushing water below me.
The seagulls squawked and screeched at one another,
Used to the human invasion of their homes.
I found that I was troubled by my own presence there,
Wishing I could jump down the rocky steep
And catch wind under my feathered wings.
I wanted to dip, dive, soar, and slide along the waves
Independent of my human skin
And all the complications that came with it.
Cool breezes and tickling green blades were all I felt
As I drifted slowly into nothingness,
Ignoring the closed-in cocoon of my human home.
As I fell asleep in Belfast, I was a bird on the sea,
Free and floating.

A Time Gone

The past, present, and future are all seen in the same time.
The past glows from above, unreachable,
Casting shadows of doubt on the ground because
We can't see where we are going.
Now we are cold and wet,
Unprepared for the depth of our destruction,
Too blinded from the sweet water that touches our eyes
And obscures our vision.
Because the future is dark and crowded.
It's made of concrete mountains.
Trees of plastic and metal are planted until
We are choking on the little oxygen we have left.
Time is running out.
We can't keep looking backward.
We won't be looking forward.
We have to look now.

Coffee and Paper

Cotton-plush sleep interrupted by sweat and sore breaths
There had to be something else here
Something worth finding that was not at Inishmore
Outside the sun was kind but the wind battled with her hair
Finding things would be a little easier with coffee
So that was the goal: cappuccino and paper
She could always find herself on paper
It was getting late and there was no place to rest her mind
Venturing back she found a secret
A circle of grand trees tangled together at the top
Wildflowers sprouted along the glowing mint grass
Clovers and moss rippled from the dark wood
She found something there in the shade of nature
Something she had been needing for a while
It was peaceful and private though she could see passersby
It still felt as though she were the only one who existed
When the storm broke the sky she was safe
Save for a random mist that dotted her journal
Coffee, paper, and a lovely storm
This was the safety she had been searching for

Cold

It was cold, and my hands were shaking.
Yet I was still able to get a clear picture
Of the city in the winter morning.
I loved seeing the balance,
Nature versus human,
The peace of the sky
Against the darkness of the Earth.
Humanity is wonderfully corrupt.
Like beautiful monsters who
Occasionally do the right thing.
I think I captured that here.
You can see the shadows that can't help but
Creep their way over the cold ground.
Despite the sun's attempt to warm us,
We are still shivering.
It's the kind of cold that envelops you
And makes you feel new and clean.
Even though so much I've found
Is tainted with our human touch.

Here

Here is the only place I've been
Always here and never there
Here is where I was born
Here is what I am
Here is never ending
Even in death I am still here
Some people say you leave
You float beyond the light and the clouds
Maybe down the water
Toward the edge of the earth
But I've never seen the edge of the Earth
So to me it is not real
Here is real
I am really here

Lady New York

Chaos follows her
Seashell hair and simple features,
She has a world inside her chest,
Pumping people through her veins,
Whole mountains towering over civilizations
She built from her flesh and mind.
There are these elements,
Moments you can see when
She opens her eyes to look at morning.
How her light and dark mingle and blend,
A beyond atmosphere that makes you feel like
You're part of something different when she talks to you.
But she has toxins in her blood too.
Man-made troubles,
Traffic in her mind on insomniac repeat.
Clouds of green and purple under her eyes.
Her breath is a swirling mess of dust, sky, and earth
Waging war on one another in harmony.
She is a contradiction.
A beautiful mess of dreams and nightmares,
Love and corruption.

Morning and Night

They were right
To be afraid of what we were capable of.
Most of us didn't believe it could happen,
That the water could run downstream.
Out of sight, out of mind, out of reach.
But we were never afraid before
Because most of us are only afraid of now.
Now: the buildings are turning to dust;
The sky is morning and night;
The ground is frozen and overcrowded.
We are afraid now,
But I'm afraid it's too late.
I'm afraid we've wasted time the same way
We've wasted this planet.

Pink Suds

We were told at a young age
That we were capable of anything.
Bred to bleed star-spangled blood, but
What if that red and blue turn poison-purple
And we can't pretend we don't know?
It is a privilege to fall in line with the rest;
Destinies manifested from past achievements
Never truly questioning anything—
Not the past tragedies that made this land "brave and free";
Grip my jaw to silence me!
Don't mention the future without
Talk of the children we must save.
The children we don't want,
The children that may not be born because
We can't figure out how to take care of you and
Your children and your children's children,
I.e., *us*!
We like it straightforward, no romance,
Tell the truth.
But only if the definition of the truth is
A mix of regurgitated opinions and mishaps
From a messy past, swept under a rug
So that we can quickly move on to the next.
Always moving. That's progress!
Spit your lies if you must.
You're not saying anything new
Because we already knew:

We were born to clean.
Clean up the messes you've been making.
But we can't get the bloodstains out of the carpet.
It's all just pushed around because it cannot be erased.
It has to go somewhere.
It's just suds and pink slush now.
It has to go somewhere.
We are awake.
We know what it is.

Sublime

I'd like to say I'm made of fire.
Because I think there is strength in burning;
There is strength in anger and pain,
And I believe I am strong.
I am lava, flame, and spark,
The smoke that seeps through your fingers and cloaks your tongue.
You cannot get close without being burned.

I'd like to say I'm made of air.
Like a ghost that leaves a chill down your spine.
I can bite and play and sting as I move with my mood.
And I believe I am more than a whisper.
I am storm, breeze, and wind.
The push and pull that gets you to where you need to go.
You cannot move without my permission.

I'd like to say I'm made of earth.
Like a connection that melts through your feet.
My body is covered in the mess of humanity,
And I believe I am peaceful with a vengeance.
I am soil, grass, and stone.
Ever growing, shifting, and quaking.
You cannot survive without me feeding you.

I'd like to say I'm made of water.
Like a wet blanket that overwhelms the life I thought I had.
My flood of emotions drowns out the noise,

And I believe that I am powerful.
I am vapor, cloud, and rain.
Partner to the wind, death to the flame, life to the earth.
You cannot live without my blessing.

I like to think I'm made of something sublime.
Something more grand and powerful
Because I want to be a secret weapon.
And I believe I am capable of more than I am allowed.
I want to be scary and large.
I want something more than my skin and bones can give me.
I want to be the Mother herself.
So I decide I am all of these things.
I play dress-up as I dance alone in the rain and wind,
Mud between my toes and a match lit so they know:
I am not to be messed with anymore.

Red Puff

If this is where I go to die
Then let me fall from this tower
And disappear in a red puff
I love this kingdom
This jungle
This pretentious place of trash and dreams
I want to struggle here
And laugh here
I want to live all the things that make me human
I want the pain
The stains of a dramatic life that was truly lived
I want to fall in and out of love and
I want to die a lovely monster
That slays all the other monsters
All the ghosts that haunt me are my friends now
And we dance an invisible dance
In my dark room with the door closed
And we cry because we can and we should
Because life is hard
But it is worth it

BODY

Angry Woman

I am an angry woman because I am a crazy woman.
    Because when these words escape my mouth, pointed and ready for battle, I will be viewed as
        Too loud and too furious.
    "Calm down, bitch! Why don't you smile more? You'd actually look pretty if you smiled."
    Because when he asked me, "Why are women so upset?" And I told him:
    "EVERYTHING."
        He didn't believe me.

I am an angry woman because I am a submissive woman.
    Because when they told me, "Boys don't like sarcastic girls,"
        I listened and swallowed my sharp tongue.
    Because while my dad packed a bag with knives, pepper spray, and a taser, my mom packed face masks and the need for male validation. "Look for schools with a better ratio of men to women.
    Women tend to overpopulate colleges nowadays." And
        suddenly a husband was just as important as a diploma.

I am an angry woman because I am a trained woman.
    Because I have been conditioned to give rather than take.
        To surrender rather than fight.
    Because while swarms of bees swell and buzz in my throat,
        all that oozes out is a honey-sweet sorry instead of the stinging truth.
    Because I have been taught to make masks.
        When I told her I was proud of my naked skin, she told me it was best to stay covered.
        So I spread the paint over my freckles; I colored my mouth:
            Pink and closed.
        My suits of armor are my eyelashes and rosy cheeks
            because being wanted by the enemy is my only purpose.
    Because I've been taught that my worth is tied to his body and his choices.
    Because they say I am free while they take my safety like a tax for daring to exist.

I am an angry woman because I am a scared woman.
    Because you strip me like the winter air strips the trees, leaving me cold and exposed.
    Because every time I look out at a crowd, I fail to distinguish friend from foe.
    Because I crave his eyes while I shrink myself.
    Because it's easier to say nothing than risk the fight that comes with a simple no.

Because when the white van or the black sedan or the silver
    SUV is parked next to me with its black glass eyes
    hiding its potential attack,
    I stumble over my shotgun seat and center console just in
    case it's hungry this time.
Because when I close my eyes, I see hands.
    My hands: white knuckles clenched around keys cutting
    into my flesh like swords.
    Your hands: grabbing, tightening, taking.
        Always taking.
Because you can.

I am an angry woman because I can't.

Body Spring

There are flowers growing from my skin.
Small sprouts and buds burst from my flesh,
Freckling my body with petals of pink.
Inviting ladybugs and bees to dance
Among my hair, following my eyes…
Or are my eyes following them?
Will they be here when I die?
As my body withers and decays,
Will the flowers die too?
Or will they continue to weave themselves
Around my hollow bones,
Burrowing into my corpse,
Making me my own lovely grave?

Losing My Strength Again

You were born with no bones in your back.
I was the one to build you up one vertebrae at a time.
Your spine was made of gelatin,
Your ribs made of string.
I waited for you to stand up for me,
But it was always my duty to hold you.
I was made to make you.
But your bones have broken.
You melted into liquid, and I could no longer keep you.
You seeped through my fingers after cloaking me in your potential.
A constant reminder of my failure.
After all I did to build you up,
After loving you and calling you strong,
You crumbled at the slightest moment of pain
And left me here alone,
Back hunched over...
I was born without any bones in my back.
I built myself up one vertebrae at a time.
I was made of gelatin and string.
And I thought I was strong.
I thought loving myself was enough,
But I betrayed me and left my body to rot.
Life challenged me, and I broke...again.

Oil Paint

Sometimes I get to be the artist.
The one who decides what goes where and why.
But lately I've given that privilege up
Into the hands of someone I thought more worthy.
Submitting to his palette knife as he spread my values,
Thalo blue and crimson red pushed back and forth
Until they turned deep violet.
It was lovely the way he marveled at my beauty,
What I was capable of.
But then he wondered what would happen
If he pushed everything, every part of me,
Out onto his canvas.
Without realizing that all my hues
Turn gray-brown when forced to mingle.
I didn't realize he didn't know what he was doing.
He didn't want the parts that weren't pretty
Even though those parts
Are what make my art so interesting.

She

I ought to sit in the dark
In a room of black nothingness
And let the fear drip off my body
One bead of sweat at a time

I am familiar with this place
This empty room with no lights
I sit, afraid of the unknown,
And crave the light to rescue me

Yet there is something else here
Sitting in the darkness with me
Something like a ghost
Or a devious angel

Something made of pink and fire
Something untamed and unbroken
Something free and burning

I ought to sit here
Waiting with the shadows
For the fear to leave me be
Wild women aren't afraid of the dark
And I am ready to unleash all that makes me She

Soft

I know that I look soft.
Rosy cheeks, round eyes, and a sweet smile.
But when you reach for my hand
You will feel my cold skin.
When you lean in to whisper
Sweet proclamations of your love,
You will be blowing wind into
A desert overcome with thorns.
When you pull me close to your side
So we can help each other stand,
You will be pulling at a volcano,
Unlovable and angry.
You will feel insignificant because
I cannot risk the vulnerability.
People say they build walls after they get hurt.
I build ecosystems.
I raise entire civilizations that wage war
On themselves while I sleep.
I am a volcano!
I need a warning sign that reads,
"Will Erupt Any Second!"
Because there is conflict inside me:
Boiling, rupturing, burning…
If I appeared on the outside
How I feel on the inside,

All you would know is crimson heat and toxic breath.
So I am not soft;
I cannot be.
I will not let you close enough to hurt me.

Today

Today I am a balloon
Forced to acknowledge
The foreign breath inside me,
Giving me the shape that says,
"It's okay because I still look like I should,"
But the party's over,
And I'm lying on the floor
Slowly losing the air and form, unnoticed,
Pulled to the ground by gravity's weight,
I am just a decoration.

Tower

The breeze is strong up here.
I'm afraid I might be blown over the edge,
But I cannot turn back now.
The sheets are all tied together,
Knots that bob and weave,
Tumbling all the way to the ground.
Every day I have to watch
As my kingdom swells with breath;
I see the streets wind like veins,
And I can never touch them.
I'm trapped up here in this tower,
But not anymore.
No longer will I be this sad girl.
I only need to slip down this rope
And disappear with all the other strangers.

Trash Can

A sheet of clear disguise—protection maybe?
And yet it doesn't protect the way you'd think.
It does not stop things from going in
But stops them from really touching the surface.
People see that clear disguise and know
I am safe to trust, an obvious sign saying,
"Dump your problems here!"
Because it looks like it's supposed to?
I look like I'm supposed to when I need to be used.
So people come, not to see me;
I am not even a second thought.
They come for many reasons,
And it just so happens I am there too.
They smudge their cloudy thoughts,
Shove papers of problems down my throat,
Force trash to collect without letting me breathe.
It's my job to listen to them without complaint.
Maybe it's what I was made to do.
I wonder, if I took this disguise off,
Would they even bother?
Would they think I was a waste?

Womb

My womb bleeds black blood, and I am all that's divine.
Destruction plagues my body, and life filters through.
Following the moon's cycle, I create a shrine,
A hallowed worship space for that bleeding black hue.
It's ready to sacrifice, a token to keep.
The ghosts that live in my womb are my children,
The ones I could love, but the price is too steep.
They steal, and they kill, yet I am the villain.
My womb is not a home for politics or men.
My womb is a battleground of blood and decay.
My spirit bleeds black, and I am born again.
My body an altar, my mind the preacher: pray!
For I am the goddess, the Mother with no kin.
The phoenix, my life an inferno without hell!
With every drop I flow, a dark river of sin.
To him a wasteland, a lair where life sits to dwell.
To me a choice, life for a life; my freedom sings,
Sung by my voice—my body is everything.

MIND

Insomnia

I can't sleep.
I can never sleep.
I cannot help but feel unwelcome
Between these four walls,
In this room,
In my bed,
My body.

You see, I've been drowning in my own self.
I am awake, and suddenly I can smell Death in my room.
I open my eyes, and he's floating over me in his dark robes,
Waiting to give me a kiss.
I'm fighting to keep that consenting yes from escaping my lips
Because I don't want to die.
He pushes on my chest until I can no longer breathe.
My heartbeat quickens;
My stomach aches,
And suddenly I'm trembling under heavy blankets,
And I can't explain
Why it feels like I have to go soon.
My body doesn't listen to my mind, and my mind doesn't
Listen to me anymore…
Whoever "me" is now.

Invader

Anxiety still feels like an invader,
A poison that wasn't there before.
And yet it's not foreign to me.
It's familiar, a home made of dread.
It gives me an edge,
But I can feel my body rejecting it.
I feel it burning up my throat,
Gurgling in my mouth,
Telling me to hurl.
No matter how hard I try
Or how badly my stomach hurts,
The poison seems to continue
As if spontaneously appearing
Just to tell me it's still here,
And it's still a part of me.

Passion

I use my hands for passion
To hold a pencil or a paintbrush and tell you what I see
To write poetry sweet and angry like my minty breath
To type up reports for grades and text my mom "I'm okay"
But lately my hands keep shaking
Maybe I drank too much coffee
Or maybe my body is aging rapidly
My cells are drying out, my blood is turning to dust as I write
Maybe it's my time
Maybe my hands can show you how lovely it has been
To be in pain this long
Because at least I know I am alive

Psychological Flexibility

I thought I was made of liquid
Or maybe a kind of sweet smoke
Fluid and flexible and finally defused
But my rigid mind is scared of this thought:
I am not vapor, wind, or free flowing
I am solid, unmoving, and stuck
So here I am, in a room of stagnant strangers,
Hoping for some sign of movement
To prove that sometimes,
Even the smallest of times,
I am of moving water and shifting clouds

Self-Pity

Self-pity is sticky.
Once you touch it, it clings to your fingers,
Gets on your face,
In your eyes,
Your hair,
Your mouth.
Self-pity will force itself down your throat until
You're choking in satisfaction at your own victimhood.
Self-pity tells you false truths based on poisoned realities.
It cloaks your eyes, mutes your mouth,
And suffocates your suffering mind.
But your hands are not so weak;
Your heart is not so defeated
That you cannot peel the layers of toxicity from your skin
And find the real truths of who and what you are.

Sad

Sleepless nights leave me searching;
Green grass and foggy thoughts
Sinking and weaving into my skin.
The night sky is dripping with secrets,
And I need to soak in all of its mystery.
As I lie on the lawn outside my house,
One drop of rain slaps my nose,
Waking me from daydreams or nightmares.
(They blend now.)
Rain pours down, telling me it's time for bed,
But if I go to bed, I'm worried I might die.
So I force my eyes to stay wide open
Even though the rain is blinding.
Through the water, I see a dark figure
Who says he is my obsidian guard,
Here to protect me from my demons.
He floats toward me, hands outstretched,
And tells me my name is Desire.
I am made of greed and pleasure.
I do what I do because I think it feels good.
And it feels great when I do what I'm not supposed to.
I'm supposed to sleep, but I crave those dark hours.
My eyes stay awake so I can taste the night.
The figure groans at my rebellion,
"Don't mistake pleasure for misery."
He covers my eyes with his hand and keeps them closed.

"Even when you are awake, you are missing out on what you really want!"
I said I desired insomnia to feel the pain I'd been living in
So I could tell that I'm alive.
"You cannot live if you keep killing yourself each night."
He envelops me in his cloak so all I know is darkness.
"This is where you're headed if you don't try!"
I grow sad at the confrontation.
He is right.
I was not living; I was dying, and I had fallen in love with my despair.
I thought that was good, that it felt good to be so sad,
Because at least that meant I could still feel.
But now I think I'd be better off if I let my guardian lull me to sleep
And found pleasure among the pillows and blankets.

Sticky

I have a brain made of honey.
I think my thoughts,
The voices in my head
Telling me false truths,
Intense truths,
That stick and fuse to my beehive mind.
Until all I am is an imposing fraud.
Until all I feel are the lies and tricks
That drip from my brain down my throat.
Until it becomes the reality.
Until it is all I can taste.

Therapy

I carry wounds
Pain over hands and words spoken long ago
Trauma is wretched and cruel
It reminds you of times of heartbreak
Warns you of signs of despair
Dread and anxiety shaking hands
As skeletons rattle and hearts can't mend
Trauma is raging against your self
It tells you stories that have been twisted with age
Never escaping the prison of thought until
My body decided it was too much too fast
And I collapsed in a heap of help and speech
Practice and apply what trinkets
Of knowledge I have collected
Over time those memories don't fade but
Over time those memories don't ache

Thinking

I think.
Constantly.
And I think that's my problem—
The thinking.
The excessive movement of thoughts buzzing in my head
Even when the rest of me has gone home for the night.

And,
I think,
It's the root of my insomnia;
The thinking after hours.

I think lots of things:
I think people are inherently tragic,
I think old lampposts are romantic;
I think coke tastes better from the glass bottle;
Alcohol tastes better left unopened and untouched,
But I think nothing tastes better than my own skin
When my blood is drowning in liquor.
I think I look my best when I feel my worst,
Which I think means I love my worst more than my best.
Which, I think, means I am broken or damaged.
I think the Sun has cured my mood, but I think winter is the most
    beautiful season.
I think I am hungry, but I think the taste of food has changed since she
    left.

I think about pain:
Who's feeling it,
Why it's important.
I think about those people that cannot feel anything, and I
Wonder
If I'd be better off, because I also think I feel too much
On top of thinking about how much I feel,
If it's too much or too little or too immature or too fake or maybe too real.

And then I think, "Is there such a thing as too real?"
But I know there is because I've felt it.
I've felt it when I'm alone, and suddenly, I can't help but think of
Every human cell in my body and become overwhelmed
By the fact that all of it is me, and yet I know none of it;
At least I think I don't.

I think the "too real" is the gunk,
The slime,
The stench wafting off all of us
And poisoning the Earth.
And that's vague, but I think you know what I mean.
I think you feel it too.

But I've also felt the "too fake,"
The insincere,
The shallow and forced human drones that only
Congest my head with angst about
The lack of authenticity around my
All-too-authentic manic-pixie person.

I think I am an abusive person.
I think I manipulate myself and others, and I think
What makes it abusive is the fact that I can see what I'm doing, and I know
I won't stop, because the truth is that
I don't think this is true.
I think I tell myself it's true so I don't have to face what's happened.
But then I think I'm writing this because I cannot face a reality
Where I am the bad guy.
So maybe I think I can't trust my own brain;
I think I'm losing my mind with each thing I think.

I thought the sickness was outside of me.
I thought it was him,
Or what he was doing to me,
Or what everything was doing to me.

Now,
I think,
Maybe,
I'm growing into myself.
That it was me instead.
I think I ruin things because I think that is my nature.
And I think they'd be better off without it.
Without the tricks and treats and tricks
That slide off me so easily and stick to them like glue.

I think there is something burnt and dark inside me...
For my whole life,
And I think it's only now that it's come out.

I think words are important, and I think
People don't understand me.
I think I like it when I intimidate people;
I think I am unlikable, and I think I am easy to talk to.
I think poorly of the majority because I think it's fair, but
I think it's maybe not actually so fair;
I think I am cool, and I think that's a lie.
I think I like conflict; I think I am a drama queen.
I think sex is important to who I am.
I think girls are magic and boys who read and listen to soft music are
    hard to find,
But I think that's objectifying.

I think the things I love are things I don't have time for;
I think time is something I have too much of or not enough of,
And I think that's been said too many times
By too many people
Complaining about too many of the same things.
Maybe I am too. Complaining about the same things, I mean.
Maybe, I think, everyone has scars like mine, and I've been
Too self-centered to notice.

I think I love people, and I think I hide when they get close.
I think I know nothing, and I think that I'm smart.
I think about being human, and I think the thinking is what defines it.
I think I am tired, and I think I can never catch up on sleep.
I think so fast my brain spins, and I think I'm sick of explaining that.

Unfocused

I have always been trapped.
Or rather, I have always trapped myself.
Long nights of stress leaping from my body,
Into my mind, and back again.
I say STOP!
And it doesn't listen.
I am unable.
And the worst part is that I think if it does stop,
Then maybe I'll lose something with it.
Maybe I need to struggle in order to be
A good writer and artist.
But everything I write is angry and sad
Because lately, I can't even stop my thoughts
From multiplying like cancer cells
Long enough for me to hear what I'm thinking.
I am in my room, and it's already a mess.
My favorite top, the one my grandmother made me,
Is crumpled on the floor, next to my dying motivation.
And it blurs my vision.
My unfocused vision…
Mirrors my unfocused mind…
Mirrors my unfocused body,
As if I am lost and unseen by the rest.

What Is Real?

Do you ever think the things you can't feel aren't real?
That maybe, somewhere in your mind, you've fabricated
This dream of some sort in order to comfort yourself,
But in reality, you're alone and scared and falling into
Your own imagination because the harness of
Your real life is too much for you now?
Because how would you know
If you truly lost your mind?

Why Are You Here?

"Why are you here today?"

Reasons rushed to the tip of my tongue,
Balancing on the edge, threatening to jump,
Committing verbal suicide—

HUSH!
Don't tell her!
Because explaining everything
Would make me too tired.
So tired that I couldn't possibly finish.
I couldn't tell her
That Fear's skeleton hand is gripping my throat.
He holds on like a noose.
Every day my own body weighs me down
As he tightens his grip.

And I'm scared.
I'm scared all the time.
There are demons in my stomach
And ghosts in my blood.
When I close my eyes, I see black cancer.
Masses: bubbled purple bombs clinging
To my heart, my brain, my skin.
When I breathe, I feel every toxin grazing my lungs
As they dwell inside me.

I can't tell my mind it's not real.
It doesn't listen to me anymore!
It's stronger than me.
It tells me every day
That I'm going to die.
I see red, tear-stained cheeks,
A shining black hearse,
And my white corpse lying still in satin and cedar.
I see everyone's pain
Because I am an open wound,
And I can't stop bleeding.

"I just don't feel well."

www.ingramcontent.com/pod-product-compliance
Lightning Source LLC
LaVergne TN
LVHW042156070526
838201LV00047BA/1426